Reading and Writin

Rhona Whiteford

Rhona Whiteford has many years' experience of teaching at preschool and primary school level, and is the author of a wide range of educational books for teachers, parents and children. She has two children.

Consultant: **Andrew Burrell**

Andrew Burrell has worked as a primary school teacher and as a lecturer at the Institute of Education, University of London, and has carried out research into the teaching of Language and Literacy.

Illustrated by **Lucy Maddison**

About this book

This book contains reading and writing activities suitable for 7- and 8-year-olds. They are based on the latest National Curriculum and National Literacy Strategy requirements for Year 3.

The activities gradually become more demanding, so it is important to start at the beginning.

The reading and writing skills taught or practised in each unit are stated at the top of the page. A note at the foot of the page tells you more about the purpose of the activities and gives advice about how to help your child with them.

Stickers are provided as a reward and as a record, and the progress chart at the back of the book gives you a useful checklist of skills.

Each unit ends with a positive comment. Encouragement from you will work wonders, so be generous with your praise!

How to help your child

- Find a quiet place to work, preferably sitting at a table.
- Work with your child occasionally, but encourage independence. Don't insist if he or she is tired or happily doing something else. Help with reading the instructions where necessary.
- Encourage your child to check his or her work.
- Look at an illustrated children's dictionary and an illustrated thesaurus together.
- Play word games with your child. Scrabble is especially helpful for reinforcing spellings.
- Look at the different kinds of language – persuasive, instructional, entertaining – used on adverts and signs.
- Read aloud to your child, and let him or her read to you.
- Encourage him or her to read a variety of material, fiction and non-fiction.
- Ask for neat, clear handwriting and attractive presentation.

Above all, be relaxed – and have fun!

Hodder Children's Books
a division of
Hodder Headline Limited

He, she or it?

I'm Lewis, and I'll help you to learn!

A **noun** is a naming word.

The boy gave the dog a bone.

A **pronoun** can be used instead.

He gave the dog a bone.

Pronouns

he   she   it   they

him   her   it   them

1 **Rewrite the captions, using pronouns instead of some of the nouns.**

The twins love sailing.

....

The twins saw Laura and Tom on the shore.

....

Sam has a ball and Sam loves to play with it.

....

....

Their parents said that their parents were having fun too!

....

....

2 Read this newspaper report.
Replace some of the nouns with pronouns.
Cross out the noun,
and write the pronoun above it.

Daily Newsbite

6th January 2001

MUM'S THE WORD ... *but what a surprise!*

by our wildlife reporter, Harry Hare

When a 10 year-old female chimp went missing from the enclosure at Tall Trees Safari Park, the keepers were very worried.

The keepers searched farmland and gardens without any sign of the chimp. But after 3 days, the chimp found the keepers! The chimp was sitting outside the gates of the Safari Park – with a new baby son whom the chimp was holding carefully. The son was gripping the mother chimp tightly. When the keepers arrived, the chimp calmly got into the van. Mother and baby are now happily home.

Brilliant! ★

Reading a play

Have you read any plays before?

This is an extract from a playscript.
Read it carefully.

RACE AGAINST TIME

Characters
Captain Jake Nimbus
Lieutenant Rex Rambo
Chief Engineer Beega Spanner

Setting
Riga Galaxy: Earthship Warrior

Rex: All systems are go, Captain!

Capt. Jake: Thank you, Lieutenant. Proceed at Full Warp, Speed 9 for the Far Galaxy.

Spanner: Captain, the engines won't take it!

Capt. Jake: They must! We have to reach the Rings of Planet Nitron in three Earth hours or we'll be caught in the biggest meteor storm of our lives.

Spanner: The ship will break up! The generators need one hour to make fuel! Our lives depend on us waiting for the power! Slow down!

Rex: The warning lights are on, Captain!

Capt. Jake: OK. We'll wait. See to it, Spanner.

Spanner: We'll outrun them all! You'll see!

Rex: Captain! The computer scanner is showing an enemy formation approaching!

Capt. Jake: Ahh! So the Zorgon War Party has found our trail. Full Warp, Speed 9, Lieutenant!

Spanner: Captain …!

Read the playscript together as many times as necessary.
Take parts, and read the speeches in appropriate voices.
(You could use three readers.)

Encourage your child to read each question carefully and
then to scan the text, looking for evidence for an answer.

Remember to answer in complete sentences.

Now answer these questions.

1 What are the characters doing?

....

2 Who is in charge?

....

3 Why must they reach Nitron quickly?

....

4 What tells you that the Captain was expecting the Zorgons?

....

5 What do you think Spanner is starting to say at the end of the extract?

....

6 Do you think this extract is exciting? Give a reason for your answer.

....

....

7 What do you hope will happen next?

....

....

Fantastic! ⭐

Thinking quickly

Some words can make you think of other words.

me → food → eat → happy

Complete these word chains as quickly as you can.

summer — hot — pool —

winter — cold — snow —

fireworks — — —

birthday — — —

wind — — —

bikes — — —

friends — — —

Try one or two of the word chains orally with your child before he starts writing. Talk about the relationships between the words. Correct spelling is not the focus of this activity, but do spell words for him if he asks you to.

Well done!

What are they saying?

When a character in a story speaks, it tells us what that character is like or what is happening in the story.

I'm the king of the jungle! You can't catch me!

1 Cross out the things you **don't** want the second lady to say.

Billy kicked his muddy football at my washing!

1 Oh, dear! I'll do it again for you.
2 I'm sorry about that!
3 He'll soon be playing for United!
4 Did it make much difference?

2 Complete the speech bubbles for these pairs of characters.

Discuss possible situations for the characters before your child starts writing the dialogue. Try out different voices for the characters.

Excellent! ★

7

Speech marks

Speech marks are placed round the words spoken by a character.

"I've written a poem," said Lewis.

Read Lewis's poem.
Put in the missing speech marks.

The park

"Have you been down to the park?"
Asked a boy whose dog was called Mark.
"You'll get such a scare
When you see what is there!"
"I was shocked!" said Mark, with a bark.

They've moved all my favourite things!
Cried a girl with her arm in a sling.
They've flattened the slide!
Yelled a boy at her side,
And they've even got rid of the swings!

I do wonder what will come next,
Said a young woman in a red vest.
Well, I'd like a pool,
Said her friend (very cool).
Yes, please! shouted all of the rest.

"Well, could it be houses?" asked Dad.
"Or a long row of shops?" cried a lad.
"I know what it will be,"
Said a girl up a tree,
"A new park! So now aren't you glad?"

Punctuation marks make a text easier to read.
Read the poem together, using a different voice for each character. Help your child to identify the words spoken by each, and to enclose them in speech marks.

Good work!

Commas

Commas can be used to separate items which are listed in a sentence.

I can see   ,   ,   and   .
I can see lions, cats, dogs and bats.

Write **and** between the last two items.

1 **Complete these sentences.**

I like buns cakes bread and crisps.

I saw elephants tigers snakes .... chimps.

I tried riding swimming judo .... rollerblading.

I would like pens paints paper .... crayons for my birthday.

2 **Now list the items from each sentence on the correct piece of paper.**
   Add two more items to each list.

Food I like	Animals I saw	Sports I tried	My birthday list
....	....	....	....
....	....	....	....
....	....	....	....
....	....	....	....
....	....	....	....
....	....	....	....

This activity will help your child to use commas correctly, and to reorganise text in a vertical form.

Wonderful! ⭐

Reading poems

Read these poems together.

A

Lion

A lion is king of the jungle,
A lion is king of the tree,
A lion is king of everything
As far as the eye can see!

B

The Lollipop Toad

How does a frog get over the road?
Do you think he knows his Green Cross Code?

When he hops from here to there,
The cars must give him an awful scare.

Maybe he knows
Of secret holes,
Or long, dark tunnels
Dug by moles.

How does a frog get over the road?
I think there must be a Lollipop Toad.
(Sam McBratney)

C

Sausages

Sausages for tea, and chips, plump and hot with crispy bits.
And shiny, tangy, tickle-your-nose tomato sauce
Like a ruby river, with sausages for tea!

Read the three poems together and discuss your responses. Read them again, concentrating on the rhythm and the descriptive language. Discuss the fact that only two of the poems rhyme.

Encourage your child to form his own opinions about what he reads, and to form personal preferences.

Now answer these questions.

1 Think about each poem.
What kind of poem is it?
Underline the correct phrase or phrases.
Use red for **Poem A**, green for **Poem B**
and blue for **Poem C**.

shape poem
story poem
senses poem   descriptive poem
riddle   funny poem
repetitive poem

2 What do you think of each poem?

A

B

C

3 Which poems rhyme? ....

4 Which is the funniest poem? ....

Write some of the funny bits here.

5 Which poem do you like best? ....

Why?

These questions require your child to search a text
for evidence to support his opinions. Help him to
organise his thoughts before he starts to write,
using words from the poems where appropriate.

Good thinking!

11

Joining sentences

A conjunction joins two short sentences to make a longer one.

This is Lewis.   This is his best friend, Len.

This is Lewis <u>and</u> this is his best friend, Len.

1   Join each pair of sentences with a conjunction.

Conjunctions

because   and
after   although
until   when   but

The sun was shining.	The sky was blue.
It was mid-morning.	We set off on our journey.
We wore thick coats.	It was freezing cold.
The match was very boring.	Our team scored two goals.
We took plenty of food.	Nobody was hungry.

2   Now rewrite one of the new sentences, using the correct punctuation.

Conjunctions make a piece of writing clearer and more fluent. When your child is writing, encourage her to reread her work and to link short sentences with conjunctions where appropriate.

Well read!

When did it happen?

Read the story extract **first of all**!

Fill each space with a word or a phrase from the box.

> in the end   first of all   at last   quickly
> in time   soon   before long   eventually
> meanwhile   finally

Ali and Jason decided to take matters into their own hands. Sam was only a puppy and he had been missing all night.

1 .... , they decided to go and look on the cliff path. But when they **2** .... set out, Jason's little sister Annie followed them secretly. It was growing hot and **3** .... she was so tired that she had to rest. **4** .... the sky went dark and huge storm clouds gathered. This was **5** .... followed by heavy rain and thunder. When it **6** .... stopped, she was soaked ... and completely lost.

7 .... , the boys had gone down to Bob's barn to shelter.

Back on the cliff, Annie was crying. But the nightmare was over **8** .... when a warm, wet nose touched her hand ...

Your child will need to read the passage very carefully. Discuss which word or phrase she should use in each space before she starts writing. (There is more than one right answer in most cases.)

Encourage your child to make her own writing more exciting by using adverbs of time like these.

Brilliant!

Planning stories

The **setting** of a story is the place where the action happens.

> **A shady spot beneath a tall tree on the African plain …**
> That's a good setting!

1 Read this description of a story setting.

> This is **my** favourite place, and I'm ready for action!

GIANT FOR HIRE

What a great strongroom I have!

The glow of the lamp makes my heaps of gold shimmer. Dark stone walls make the mountains of coins look even bigger. The only pieces of furniture are my counting table and a great oak chair, big enough for three ordinary giants. I keep my treasure chest open a little so that the jewels can peep out and twinkle at me, but I have no windows for strangers to peep through. The great black door is bolted with iron! Ha, ha, ha!

Describe **your** favourite place.

....

....

Describe a setting for your favourite character.

....

....

Read the description of the giant's strongroom carefully, and talk about what might happen there.

An awareness of setting will make your child's writing more colourful. To develop his vocabulary, talk about the settings of his favourite stories, films or television serials. (The setting may change two or three times.)

If a story **begins** in an interesting way, you want to read on.

> **One afternoon, I was snoozing quietly when I heard a strange hissing noise ...**

Sssssss

2 **Read these story ideas.**
Write the beginning of a story for each one.

An underwater adventure with dolphins

....

....

An unusual teatime

....

....

A good **ending** brings a story to a satisfying close.

> **... and so I said goodbye to the electric snake, and settled down under my tree again.**

3 **Read these story ideas.**
Write a story ending for each one.

A lost child is found

....

....

Aliens invade your school

....

....

A good story needs a structure, and this activity will help your child to generate ideas for ways of beginning and ending. Make some suggestions, e.g. *One beautiful, starry night, I ... .*

Fantastic!

15

Let's find out

Find out about these topics before you go!

You have won a fabulous ten-day family holiday on a tropical island off the coast of Africa!

A the weather   F sea creatures
B air travel   G the countryside
C sea travel   H the people
D popular sports   I the food
E land creatures

**Choose some books to help you to research the topics.
Write the letter of the topic next to the book.**

Some of the books may be useful for more than one topic!

Whales and Porpoises

Coral Reefs

TROPICAL FISH

Stories Around the World AFRICA

Tropical Butterflies

BRITISH Butterflies

ANTARCTICA

Warm Seas

EARTHQUAKES

ISLAND LIFE

Canoeing for Beginners

SURFING THOSE WAVES

Travelling by Plane

AFRICAN FOOD

HANG-GLIDING MADE EASY

BRITISH WEATHER

TROPICAL WEATHER

Swimming for Me

Tropical Reptiles

POLAR BEARS I'VE KNOWN

Read the list of topics carefully, and discuss which of the reference books might be helpful. Talk about the likely contents of each.

Encourage your child to use reference books in the children's library if she needs to find information.

Well spotted!

Making notes

Read the information.
Write key words or phrases which
will remind you of the facts.

Lions!

African plains
Sandy coat
Meat-eaters
Prides
Hunters

Parrots

The parrot family includes parakeets, cockatoos, macaws and
many more brightly coloured birds. All have strong, curved
beaks and grasping toes with which they can hold food. They
eat fruit, nuts, grain and nectar, and some even eat small
animals. Some live in jungles, some in open fields and some on
mountains. All parrots mate for life and both parents care for
the young. They live in huge flocks, except in the breeding
season. Parrots are found in all tropical regions of the world.

Parrots

....

....

....

This activity will develop your child's concentration
and help her to analyse information.

Read the passage with your child and help her to
identify new vocabulary and to find important
information (habitat, appearance, feeding,
breeding, social habits, etc.)

Well done! ⭐

17

Ways of writing

When you write a message, think carefully about who is going to read it. This will affect the way you write it!

Remember my sweets!

Please don't forget the sweets, dear Mum.

1 **Write a message …**

… to a friend to arrange a meeting.

… to yourself to remind yourself about a special event in the holidays.

… to a favourite adult to ask for something.

… to a teacher to explain about your child's illness (pretend to be a parent!)

Writing styles vary according to the person who is going to read the writing, and the purpose of that writing. The activities on these two pages will help your child to think about this.

Talk about appropriate language for the messages before he starts to write.

2 Read this news report.

News reports give information. Comics are for entertainment.

DAY OUT DISASTER

A school trip turned into a terrible tragedy today as a lorry crashed into a coach carrying 30 children home from the seaside. Unfortunately, 3 children were badly hurt and 27 were slightly injured. A police spokesperson said that they weren't wearing seatbelts. The parents are devastated and angry.

Underline the serious words and phrases, and then write them here.

3 Now read these two pages from a comic.

Write the funny words and phrases here.

ZIPPY

HELLOEEE! CAN I JOIN IN?

GOODBYEEEE!

ZOOM!

ARRRGH!

TWANG!

TEE HEE!

The pieces of writing on this page are typical of printed texts for a mass readership. One is formal and informative, the other for entertainment. Talk about the contrasting styles and vocabulary of the two texts.

Well written!

19

Collecting words

Think of two more words to write on each pod.
Use a thesaurus if you like.

These words will be helpful when you are writing poems and stories.

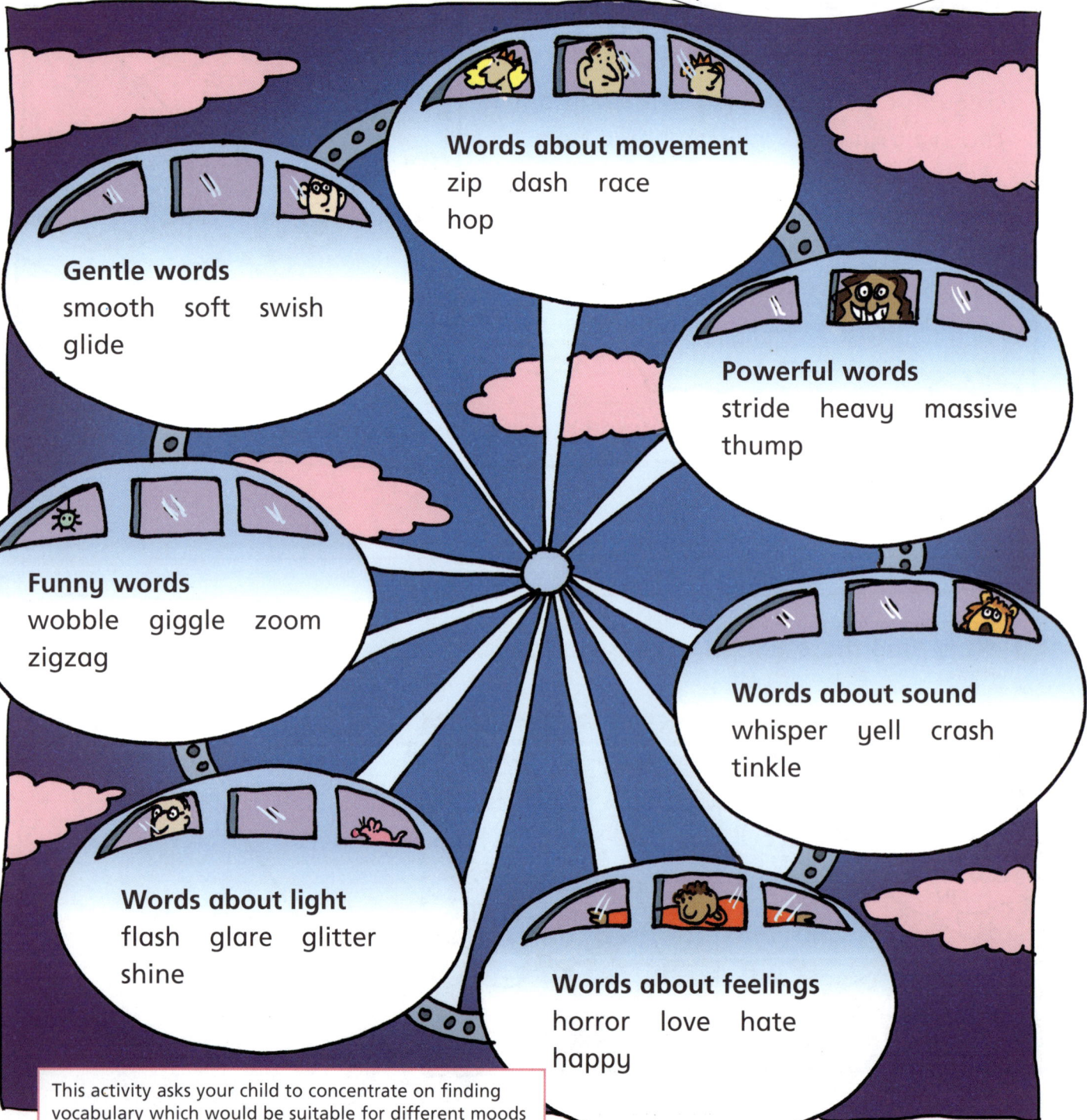

Words about movement
zip dash race
hop

Gentle words
smooth soft swish
glide

Powerful words
stride heavy massive
thump

Funny words
wobble giggle zoom
zigzag

Words about sound
whisper yell crash
tinkle

Words about light
flash glare glitter
shine

Words about feelings
horror love hate
happy

This activity asks your child to concentrate on finding vocabulary which would be suitable for different moods of creative writing. You may find that that the words she chooses stimulate ideas for poems or stories.

Work together on the activity, making notes as you talk.

20

Excellent!

Writing a shape poem

Complete this shape poem.

You may want to use some of the words you collected on page 20 or the ones on this page!

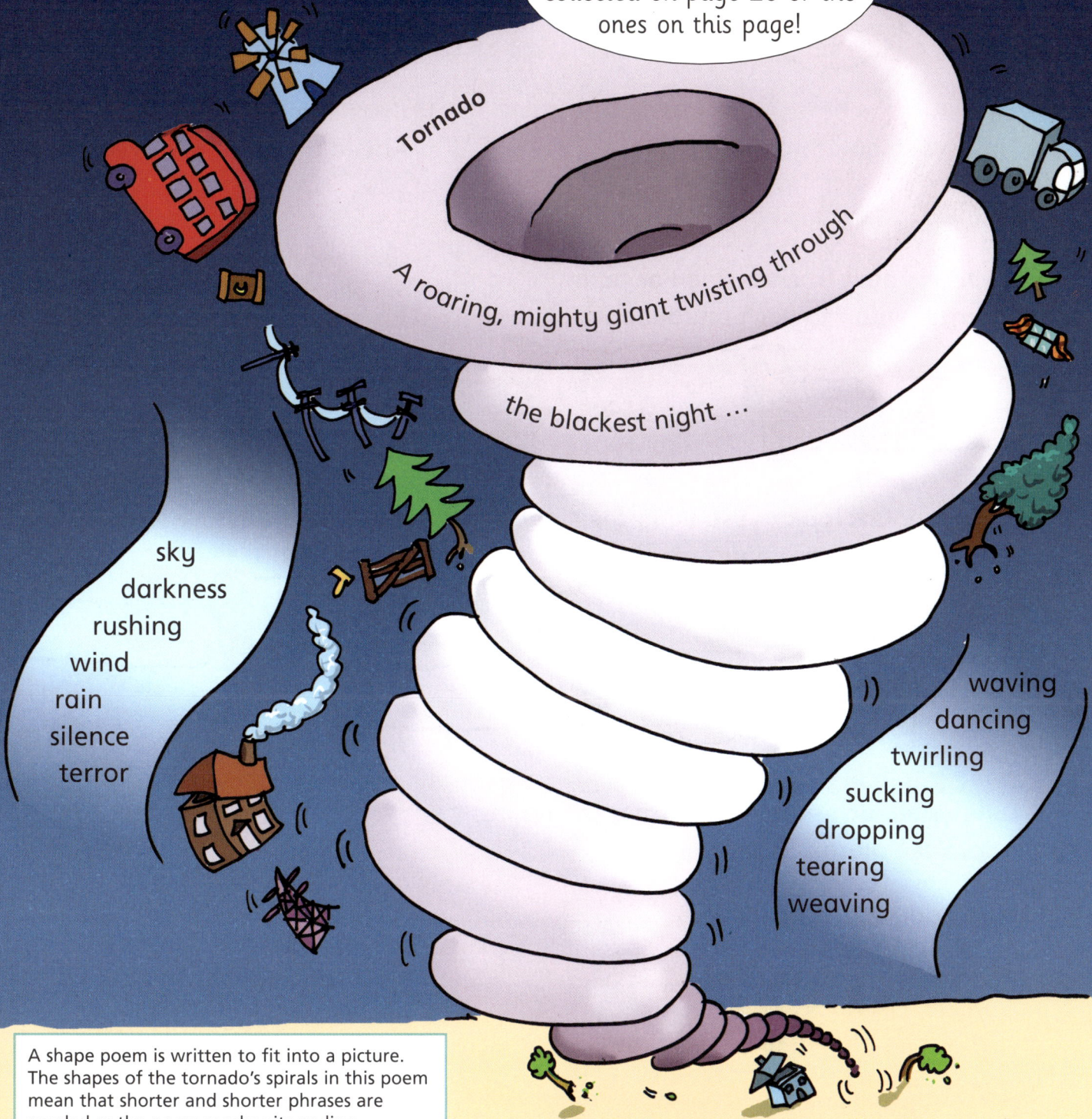

Tornado

A roaring, mighty giant twisting through

the blackest night ...

sky
darkness
rushing
wind
rain
silence
terror

waving
dancing
twirling
sucking
dropping
tearing
weaving

A shape poem is written to fit into a picture. The shapes of the tornado's spirals in this poem mean that shorter and shorter phrases are needed as the poem reaches its ending.

Encourage your child to read her poems aloud; performing in front of an audience will increase her confidence and help her to judge the effectiveness of her work.

Good work!

More than one

lion

This is a **singular noun**.

lions

If there are more than one, we need a **plural noun**.

1 Write **s** next to each singular noun.
Write **p** next to each plural noun.

Be careful! Not all plural nouns end in **s**!

women   sun   child   trees

2 Some nouns look the same in the singular and the plural forms.
Write **b** next each noun which is both singular and plural.

deer   children   girls   sheep

mice   toys

3 Rewrite each sentence, putting the nouns into the plural.

You may need to change other words, too!

The dog ate its biscuit. ....

The boy ran to the shop. ....

The child played in his garden. ....

The bird flew to the tree. ....

Most nouns can be made plural by adding *s*. Others (e.g. *mouse – mice*) have an irregular plural. A few nouns (e.g. *deer*) are the same in the singular and the plural forms. Your child will gradually master these variations as he uses them in speech and in writing.

Some plural nouns are **group nouns**.

We are all **cats**!

Flowers

....

....

....

....

....

4 List each of these nouns under the correct group noun. Add one more.

buttercups   penguins   angel fish   seagulls

tulips   ostriches   goldfish   pilchards

roses   sharks   daffodils   robins

Birds

....

....

....

....

....

Fish

....

....

....

....

....

5 Write the correct group noun at the top of each list. Underline the odd one out.

....	....	....	....
trainers	green	pianos	computers
slippers	red	guitars	lions
slip-ons	violet	radios	wolves
scarves	orange	violins	leopards
sandals	paper	recorders	cougars

Some plural nouns (e.g. *birds*) are group nouns; they act as 'headings' for a number of other nouns. Extend this activity by brainstorming nouns which could go under the headings *Vegetables*, *Cars* or *Footballers*.

A **collective noun** describes a group of similar things.

a pride of lions

6 **Look at these collective nouns.**

 bunch

 flock

 library

 herd

 herd

 swarm

 class

 fleet

 gaggle

 string

 herd

 shoal

 bunch

 litter

 flock

 pack

 forest

 school

 sheaf

 pack

Write the collective noun for each of these.

a .... of whales

a .... of children

a .... of birds

a .... of kittens

a .... of beads

a .... of trees

a .... of ships

a .... of bees

Most children are interested in collective nouns – especially the more unusual ones (e.g. *a murder of crows*). Keep a list of collective nouns, adding to it as you find examples.

7 **Complete each sentence with a collective noun.**

Sam ate a huge .... of bananas.

The .... of fish glided smoothly through the water.

The .... of elephants plodded down to the river.

Gary gave his mother a .... of flowers.

8 **Write a caption for each of these pictures.**

a pack of wolves

....

....

9 **Write two sentences containing collective nouns.**

Wonderful! ⭐

What are they like?

An **adjective** describes a **noun**.

a <u>**young**</u> **lion**

I'm also **handsome, clever** and **modest**!

---

1 Underline each adjective in blue, and each noun in red.

a fierce lion

a wet child

a delicious ice cream

a blazing sun

---

2 Complete each phrase with two of these adjectives.

jiggling   slimy   hairy   dark   huge   wide   terrible   toothy   lovely
pink   quiet   mysterious   purple   spotty   noisy   creepy

a ....,
.... jelly

a ....,
.... foot

a ....,
.... grin

a ....,
.... present

---

3 Complete each sentence with an adjective.

The huge, ... dog barked loudly.

My mum buys .... , sticky buns.

Extend this activity by collecting adjectives to describe family members, pets or food. Encourage your child to use interesting adjectives in her writing, using a thesaurus if she wishes.

Brilliant! ⭐

Writing a play

Plays are written in **dialogue**, like this.

Lewis: Good day, old pal!
Len: Where are we going?
Lewis: Aha! Wait and see!

Write a short piece of dialogue for these two characters.

A bear with magic powers

Name:

A lost child

Name:

Where does the action take place?

Is the weather a problem?

Where are they going?

What time of day is it?

How did they meet?

Word bank amazing explore frightened discover wonder

Bear: ....

Child: ....

Bear: ....

Child: ....

Bear: ....

Child: ....

Finish the playscript on a sheet of paper, writing for your child as she dictates. Use words from the word bank, adding your own ideas. Read the completed playscript together, each taking the part of one of the characters.

Great ideas!

Which verb?

I **roar** loudly sometimes.

I can also **whisper** quietly.

1 **Write each verb under the correct heading.**

tear   gobble   whisper   run

like

gallop

swim

chomp

cry

shriek

Ways of speaking

trot   roar

shout

Ways of moving

dance

ask

love

stroll

fear

yell   nibble

hate   chatter

Ways of feeling

jump

creep

Ways of eating

crawl   hope

talk   climb   slurp

glide   suck

gossip   chew   natter

slither

Choosing verbs carefully can make writing more expressive. For example, *cried* or *whispered* can convey meaning more accurately than *said*.

Talk about the different kinds of verb you meet in stories.

2 **Rewrite each sentence using a different verb. Draw a picture.**

You could use some of the verbs from page 28.

Dad **ate** his food quickly.

The horse **jumped** over the last fence.

My baby brother **crawled** away.

Our dog **barks** all day.

Our teacher **speaks** for hours and hours.

The Prime Minister **appeared** on television.

Extend this activity by saying a simple sentence and asking your child to change the verb.
Then have another turn yourself. See how many verbs you can use in the same sentence.

Fantastic! ⭐

Skills test

Use this framework
to plan a story.

I have started
making the notes
for you!

Title

Setting
a snowy land
fir trees   hills

Time
night
moonlight
stars out

Weather
cold
clear
bright
dry

Characters

Beginning

Main events

1

2

3

Ending

Good ideas!

Stories need careful planning. Discuss your child's
suggestions, and encourage her to look back at
pages 14-15 for ideas.

Now write the story here.

Write the story you planned on page 30, or try one of these ideas.

The worst winter
My favourite things
Space pirates
The treasure hunt
The best thing about school

Title

Encourage your child to think carefully about the structure of her story before starting to write, and to consider her reader. She should be able to find some interesting vocabulary by looking back through this book.

Give her a time limit, but don't treat the activity too seriously. You can use the completed story to see how much your child's writing has improved since she started the book.

Good thinking!

Answers

Pages 2-3

1 The twins love sailing.
They saw Laura and Tom on the shore.
Sam has a ball and he loves to play with it.
Their parents said that they were having fun too!

2 When a 10 year-old female chimp went missing from the enclosure at Tall Trees Safari Park, the keepers were very worried.

They searched farmland and gardens without any sign of her. But after 3 days, she found them! She was sitting outside the gates of the Safari Park – with a new baby son whom she was holding carefully. He was gripping her tightly. When the keepers arrived, she calmly got into the van. Mother and baby are now happily home.

Pages 4-5

1 They are launching their spaceship.
2 Captain Jake Nimbus is in charge.
3 They want to miss a meteor storm.
4 He says, "So the Zorgon War Party has found our trail."
5-7 *free choice*

Page 6

free choice

Page 7

1-2 *free choice*

Page 8

"They've moved all my favourite things!"
Cried a girl with her arm in a sling.
"They've flattened the slide!"
Yelled a boy at her side,
"And they've even got rid of the swings!"

"I do wonder what will come next,"
Said a young woman in a red vest.
"Well, I'd like a pool,"
Said her friend (very cool).
"Yes, please!" shouted all of the rest.

Page 9

1 I like buns, cakes, bread and crisps.
I saw elephants, tigers, snakes and chimps.
I tried riding, swimming, judo and rollerblading.
I would like pens, paints, paper and crayons for my birthday.

2

Food I like	Animals I saw
buns	elephants
cakes	tigers
bread	snakes
crisps	chimps
free choice	*free choice*

Sports I tried	My birthday list
riding	pens
swimming	paints
judo	paper
rollerblading	crayons
free choice	*free choice*

Pages 10-11

1 *Red*: repetitive poem
Green: funny poem
Blue: shape poem, senses poem, descriptive poem
2 *free choice*
3 A B
4 *free choice*
5 *free choice*

Page 12

1 and
when
because
until
but
2 *Make sure there is only one capital letter and one full stop.*

Page 13

1-8 *Make sure each answer makes sense in the context of the sentence.*

Pages 14-15

1-3 *free choice*

Page 16

Ask your child to explain why the chosen books are relevant to the topics.

Page 17

Check that your child has noted key facts, e.g. brightly coloured birds.

Pages 18-19

1 *Make sure that each message is written in an appropriate style for the reader.*
2 disaster   terrible tragedy
unfortunately   badly hurt
slightly injured   devastated and angry
3 HELLOEEE GOODBYEEE ZOOM ARRRGH TWANG TEE-HEE

Page 20

Make sure that each of the chosen words is suitable for its category.

Page 21

Make sure that the poem uses suitable vocabulary and fits the space.

Pages 22-25

1 *s*: sun   child
p: women   trees
2 *b*: deer   sheep
3 The dogs ate their biscuits.
The boys ran to the shops.
The children played in their gardens.
The birds flew to the trees.

4

Flowers	Birds	Fish
buttercups	penguins	angel fish
tulips	seagulls	goldfish
roses	ostriches	pilchards
daffodils	robins	sharks
free choice	*free choice*	*free choice*

5 Shoes; scarves *should be underlined*
Colours; paper *should be underlined*
Instruments; radios *should be underlined*
Animals; computers *should be underlined*

6 a school of whales   a string of beads
a class of children   a forest of trees
a flock of birds   a fleet of ships
a litter of kittens   a swarm of bees

7 bunch
shoal
herd
bunch

8 a pack of wolves   a flock of sheep
a gaggle of geese
a herd of cows/ cattle

9 *free choice*

Page 26

1 *Blue*: fierce wet delicious blazing
Red: lion child ice cream sun
2 *Make sure that the chosen adjectives suit the pictures.*
3 *free choice*

Page 27

free choice

Pages 28-29

1 Ways of:

speaking	moving	eating	feeling
shriek	swim	chomp	like
yell	run	gobble	love
cry	gallop	nibble	hate
roar	trot	slurp	fear
ask	tear	suck	hope
shout	jump	chew	
whisper	creep		
talk	dance		
chatter	crawl		
gossip	stroll		
natter	slither		
	glide		
	climb		

2 *free choice*

Pages 30-31

Look for interesting, relevant ideas, original vocabulary and correct grammar and punctuation.